Lord of My Land

5 Steps to Homeownership

JAY MORRISON

Published by: Good 2 Go Publishing
Typesetting: Mychea
Copyright © Jay Morrison, 2016
Jay Morrison
Founder & CEO
The Jay Morrison Brand
1170 Peachtree Street
Suite 1246
Atlanta, GA 30309
Office: 1-844-JOIN JMA
Fax: 1-888-847-5915
www.JayMorrison.net

ISBN # 978-1-943686-58-2

Please note that much of this publication is based on personal experience and anecdotal evidence. Although the author and publisher have made every reasonable attempt to achieve complete accuracy of the content in this book, they assume no responsibility for errors or omissions. Also, you should use this information as you see fit, and at your own risk. Your particular situation may not be exactly suited to the examples illustrated here; in fact, it's likely that they won't be the same, and you should adjust your use of the information and recommendations accordingly.

Any trademarks, service marks, product names or named features are assumed to be the property of their respective owners, and are used only for reference. There is no implied endorsement if we use one of these terms.

CONTENTS

Lord of My Land!

Introduction

In 2011, I spent time reflecting and trying to find my "why" my purpose and what I loved about real estate. This led me back to the emotion and level of accomplishment I felt when purchasing my first home. Growing up in poverty, being a high school dropout, and making mistakes in my youth landed me in a considerable amount of trouble until I turned my life around in my mid-twenties. That moment was a validation point for me, I was on the right track headed in a positive direction. Coming from the environment in which I grew up, living below the poverty line, being on welfare and being a young man with no direction in life, to purchasing multiple properties is something of great value to me.

There is a substantial amount of statistics on how real estate and homeownership affects people as individuals, families, communities, and as a country. I have seen firsthand how the minority community is in search of leaders within the real estate acquisition and homeownership arenas.

I decided if we can teach adults while catching our youth early on, we can create change in bridging the wealth gap created by homeownership. A major part of this transition is to alter the way we look at real estate. The scope should change from complication and fear to hope and inspiration. I want it to be understood that it's much easier to buy a home than many may think. With that in mind, I set out to write this book, which outlines a step-by-step guide to home-ownership.

In 2012, I launched a series of speaking engagements based off of my first book, Hip Hop 2 Homeowners, visiting high schools to teach the students about real estate and financial principles. Everything from credit and FICO scores to the precise definition of a mortgage was game for discussion. I felt that in reaching out to the high schools and integrating fun with knowledge, we could drive home the importance of financial literacy.

Using a DJ to help open up interaction and driving engagement through games, music, and contests, this information was a hit! This fruitful educational series reached 30,000 students during the first year and is still active. It is a true passion of mine to bring something innovative to the table while empowering and educating our youth. We have had success at alternative schools, prep schools, public and private schools. The program has been a universal success and I continue to get booked using www.JayMorrison.net.

During the first speaking engagement at a New Jersey high school on February 10 2012, I spontaneously shared a personal story. Since then, I always make it a point to include this story, which is the motivation for the title of this book.

It's the story of the day I pulled up to the first two-family home I owned (this was the second property I had purchased; the first house was a gift to my mother). I lived in one unit and rented out the other to a tenant, a middle-aged Caucasian woman with two children. At the young age of 25 years old, I pulled up in my Range Rover, black with cream interior and black trim, bumping Lil' Wayne and enjoying my day. I was making money in the mortgage and real estate industry and things were going well for me.

As my tenant's daughters were playing on the lawn, they yelled, "The landlord is here! The landlord is here!" That was one of those "A-ha" moments for me, and suddenly the day seemed brighter, I could hear birds chirping. I was Lord of My Land! That's where the term comes from. We say "landlord," but rarely consider what the word actually implies. Typically, we think of a landlord as the person we see depicted in sitcoms on TV or in movies. Usually it is a middle-aged white guy, the person you pay rent to or call about a leaking faucet. So when I was called "landlord," it sunk in I was the Lord of My Land. I was the owner and the highest authority of this property. After pondering on it, I realized this was big, this was huge. Very few people in the minority community, particularly those with my background, have the opportunity to own property. My people usually prefer to blow their money on cars or other liabilities, and real estate is not even on the radar.

The Realtor made $13,000 on commission just for showing me that house. That's when I decided to get my real estate license. I mean, my agent only went to the property twice! I did most of the work and the agent received a nice, fat check. Then on the Housing and Urban Development (HUD) form, I saw all the fees the buyer pays versus the money the seller pockets. The seller made $100,000 after only owning the property for 10 years. Imagine buying a two-family home, renting out both units for a decade, then selling it at a six-figure profit. I thought if I can buy 9 more properties, rent them out, and sell them in 10 years for a profit of $100,000, I could be a millionaire by the age of 35!

My experience with that property had a lasting impact on me because of the lessons I learned which drove me to take my real estate career to the next level. The fact that I could earn rental income from a property when positioned the right way, earn appreciation in equity which results in cash, as well as be able to take advantage of tax write-offs were valuable realizations for me. What held the most weight overall for me, however, is the intangible feeling and responsibility of being Lord of My Land. It positioned me in a better status and even put me in recorded history in its own way. When you own property, you are recorded in the town's tax records. You are officially Lord of that Land, anyone on your property is subject to your authority.

These are the reasons why I believe everyone should understand how simple the principle is. Everyone should be knowledgeable on the home buying process, the required strategy and mindset that's needed to purchase your first home. In my experience as a real estate developer, strategy coach and mentor we often get caught up in the higher level conversations regarding real estate investing, flipping and building a portfolio with commercial properties. I felt it would be more beneficial to come back to my roots, providing everyone the simplest, most inspiring blueprint on how to become Lord of Your Land and buy your first home.

Understanding the Importance of Homeownership

Individual

Whether you are single, married, or engaged, it is important to own property in order to start building wealth and set yourself up for the home's appreciation, or increase in value over time. It's a great financial play for an individual. There are also many tax benefits in owning a home. Items such as your mortgage interest and closing costs are tax deductible. If you own a multi-unit, some of the maintenance and repairs are tax deductible as well. Even property depreciation is tax deductible. There are many more tax incentives, but I'm sure you are getting the picture. Owning a property just makes a lot of sense financially.

Bear in mind if you are a renter, whether you are living with somebody or you rent a property, you can spend anywhere from $1,000 up to $5,000 per month and find yourself living in a beautiful penthouse or regular middle class apartment. However, no matter what you spend on rent during the year, none of it is tax deductible, or sets you up for future appreciation or equity, nor does it put you in a position of ownership. All it does is keep a roof over your head. So, if you could own a home for the same amount you pay in rent every month or perhaps a little more, it's worth the sacrifice. It may mean eating out a little less frequently, buying fewer clothes, or just cutting back on other costs for the sake of owning. The reward is investing into your own future as opposed to somebody else's by continuing to rent.

Homeownership is the best chess move you can make because we all need a roof over our heads, so why not put yourself in the position of owning that roof instead of renting it and metaphorically and theoretically throwing your hard earned money away The reward of ownership will be an investment into your future rather than into someone else's family legacy. Long term, it puts you in a better financial position.

From a renting standpoint, all you get back is a security deposit and typically not 100% because the landlords always figure out a way to   retain some of that deposit money. Let's say you live somewhere for 5 years paying $1,000 a month, that is $60,000 over that time period.

$$\underset{\text{(Cost of Rent)}}{\$1,000} \times \underset{\text{(Months in a year)}}{12} = \underset{\text{(Total Rent in 1 year)}}{\$12,000} \times \underset{\text{(Years)}}{5} = \underset{\text{(Total Rent in 5 years)}}{\$60,000}$$

When you get ready to move, not one single penny goes with you to the next place. All you did was help the landlord pay off his mortgage.

As an individual, aside from your education, owning a business, and starting a family, there is no bigger personal goal you can have than owning the space you live in. With that said, it's important for you to take the proper steps to put yourself in a position of becoming Lord of Your Land.

Family

Homeownership is key for families because a lot of family wealth is passed down through property. Many families are able to provide their children with a college education or help them start their first business and support their careers, along with setting up for their retirement, all through leveraging the equity on their property by refinancing and accessing lines of credit. All of this enables them to meet certain financial needs. Being Lord of Your Land and having family owned property, becomes part of your family's legacy. If we do this today in 2016, we would be helping to set up the legacies for our children's families and then their children's and so on for however long it is passed down.

Now, looking at it from the opposite end, if you rent for 30 years, when you are ready to retire you will not be able to tap into that 30 years' worth of rental payments. If, for example, you paid $1,000 rent monthly for that amount of time, you paid $360,000 in rent.

$$\$1{,}000 \times 12 = \$12{,}000 \times 30 = \$360{,}000$$
(Cost of Rent) (Months in a year) (Total Rent in 1 year) (Years) (Total Rent in 5 years)

That's over a quarter million dollars! To think some of us pay $1,500, $2,000, and even $2,500 in rent every month.

$$\$2,500 \times 12 = \$30,000 \times 30 = \$900,000$$

(Cost of Rent)   (Months in a year)   (Total Rent in 1 year)   (Years)   (Total Rent in 5 years)

The latter figure adds up to almost $1 million in rent when you could have paid off a $500,000 mortgage in full and had that much equity built in that home for you, your spouse or your kids to be able to utilize. Not to mention the extra $400,000 you would have kept in your pockets!

Being lifetime renters, we do a disservice to our families by not leaving them anything substantial in terms of property, land, or the benefits of actually having owned in that time period. We do not set a good example due to lack of understanding homeownership and falling short of taking the necessary steps to conquer the fear of educating ourselves to pursue owning our own homes. We plant the seeds of fear and misconception that real estate is not for us (our type of people or our type of family). Real estate and ownership is for everybody! That's why I have provided a blueprint for homeownership and outlined the necessary steps to becoming Lord of Your Land.

An important byproduct of owning a home that affects individuals and families is a renewed boost of character, as well as a newfound sense of responsibility. Responsibility is a fundamental trait required for anyone who wants to be great and do anything substantial. Some people avoid taking the steps to owning a home because they shy away from the responsibility of maintaining the home and prefer to pass that accountability on to the landlord. In doing that, the landlord not only inherits the responsibility, but also receives what you pay them in rent, in addition to the appreciation on the property. In essence, what starts out as 'passing the buck' to dodge liability, is actually irresponsible and sets a bad example for our children.

"If I buy a house, I will be responsible if the ceiling leaks."

Yes! And if the air condition conks out…and if the toilet breaks…and if the pipe bursts, as well as finding someone to mow the lawn. It's a shame that people miss out on the advantages of being a homeowner because they are afraid of the responsibility. In order to achieve your desired goals and reach greatness, you have to embrace the obligations and responsibility that come with those choices. The homeowner who inherits that property and the risk also inherits the roof and the rent check. When your family realizes they are the owners of that property, they will manage it better, take care of the home and the land out of pride and protect what is theirs.

In an area where more families own the homes they live in, they take better care of their property and also their community because of the sense of pride in ownership. You want to protect what is yours. Think about driving rental cars, the concept applies. People abuse rentals and will do things in a rental that they never would in their own car. Some are totally irresponsible with their rental car just as there are people who are totally irresponsible with their rental property because it isn't theirs and they don't care if they run it into the ground. There's no incentive to keep it up. Of course, there are plenty of tenants who do a great job of caring for the property they rent which is great for the morale of the family, but in the end you're doing a great job keeping up a property that's not yours. It's your landlord's!

This is of utmost importance if we're going to put that kind of effort into a property, our home life, and our living circumstance, we should be benefitting from those efforts by gaining the equity, residual income of a rental and potential tax breaks from our property. Statistics show the many social benefits of homeownership and stable housing for families and their children. According to research published in April 2003 by the Neighborhood Reinvestment Corporation, comparing the children of homeowners to those of renters, children of homeowners:

- Are 25% more likely to graduate from high school
- Are 116% more likely to graduate from college
- Are 20% less likely to become teenage mothers
- Have 9% higher math scores
- Have 7% higher reading scores
- Have 3% fewer behavior problems

- Are 59% more likely to own a home within 10 years of moving from a parent's household Community

Community

When you see gentrification happening and rising rents in the community, its purpose is to push out the lower income demographic to invite in a higher income demographic because they can afford loftier rental rates. In those situations, if you are not a tenant, but owner of a property, you would have power and a say-so in what happens in your community.

For example, if there were 30 of us who own property in an area where big businesses or the government want to come in and gentrify the area, they would have to come through us. Even if they implemented eminent domain, which is the government's right to take over property for certain projects, they would have to pay us top dollar based on market value. We would also have the right to fight for it in court. It boils down to the fact that as a property owner you have more rights than you do as a renter. As a tenant, you wouldn't have any say-so, in other words, you wouldn't have a voice. Only property owners have a say in their community and the direction in which it goes.

Also, in communities where there is a strong presence of homeownership, there is less violence, less gang activity, less litter, and less trash. There is a substantial difference in places where homeowners are responsible and have a sense of pride, due to the better level of care given to maintain their community. It invokes a different culture and environment, creating a positive influence for their children and members of that community.

Every time a new homeowner becomes a part of a neighborhood, they boost the economy in that area. They require the services of carpenters, painters, electricians, plumbers, landscapers, and others who serve as a stimulus for the community and its workers. Homeownership, as a benefit of the community, drives revenue. When a property is empty, there are no taxes being paid on that property. Once

...meone moves in, tax dollars are being driven into that repair, schools and rioting, owners are less vandalism and ...mmunity. If all ...u are the person ...ample) without ...t, but don't own ...ink twice about ...s. As a property ...d with owning. ... you have owned a home, y... ...meowners have. Homeowners know what it feels like to purchase your first home, maintain a home and go through the crunch of a mortgage crisis. They will be more empathetic to other homeowners going through the same things. I know if more people owned property, there would not be so much destruction during uprisings, because those involved would spend more time thinking about how the guy felt on the other side.

I understand everyone is not going to own, however everyone should know how to own and be able to make an educated decision which works best for them.

Country

The country had a mortgage meltdown due to the predatory lending of mortgage companies, but it was also equally due to the lack of education of America's home buyers. If more people knew about real estate, the home buying process, how and why they should buy, and the trends of the market, we would have more homeowners. You don't buy overpriced properties or get into a bidding war paying more than the property is worth. You don't act aggressively in a seller's market, you don't finance a house 100% and squeeze yourself to the limit with what you can afford. You don't get adjustable rate mortgages hoping to one day get a fixed interest rate. The housing crisis could have been avoided altogether, or it would have been much less severe, had consumers been better informed. Everyone needs a place to live, so essentially homeownership touches every life. Unfortunately, homeownership is not taught in the school systems.

"Since it's not taught in grade school, high school or college, where does one learn how to buy a house?"

How do you learn to buy a house if it's never taught? That means only the wealthy or those who have had established property owners in their family or others around them who are willing to mentor them through the process have the benefit of being educated on the process and can take advantage of it.

Platforms at the Jay Morrison Academy are priceless because we are able to educate the masses on something that is not common knowledge and there is no system within our country which provides this common knowledge. You will know how to dissect a frog, learn the angles of an obtuse triangle and how to play dodge ball in gym, yet graduate from high school without knowing anything about credit, what financing is and how to buy real estate. Even those who are homeowners could stand to be more educated in real estate as we create wealthier families. We can create more taxpayers, which will introduce more revenue for cities and crime rates will plummet as a residual effect within our country as a whole. More people will be put to work: contractors, painters, plumbers, mortgage lenders, title agents, inspectors and real estate agents.

If American homeowners had this Five Step Guide prior to the foreclosure crisis during 2007-2009, we probably could have avoided such a catastrophe with more educated homeowners who understood the entire home buying process.

Step 1
Finding Your Path,
Fighting Your Fear

Fighting your fear

One of the most common things I have seen when it comes to people owning their first property is the fear of being rejected. This fear can arise when purchasing your second or third property, depending on the experience you had buying your first property. We have already covered the fear of owning a home due to the amount of responsibility that comes with it, but there is also a fear of not being approved. People don't even try because they think they will not get approved for the loan. They make up a ton of excuses in their heads instead of allowing themselves to take the path to homeownership.

- 'I'm too young.'
- 'I'm too old.'
- 'I don't make enough money.'
- 'My credit is screwed up.'
- 'I don't have enough saved.'

The first step to being a homeowner is putting all of your excuses to the side! Get rid of those pessimistic thoughts about your credit, your income, and leaky faucets one day. You must have a paradigm shift into thinking a different way. When you think about the glass being half empty or half full, how do you see it?

Think about it…fill up a glass halfway and give it to two people. One will say, "Man, this glass is half full." The other person comments, "This glass is half empty," looking at it as if something good is going away. The same outlook can be taken on homeownership. Instead of saying, "I'm not even going to try because I won't get approved," try, "I may not be ready yet, but I'm halfway there."

"I can give you every single step, but if you lack the motivation to own a home …you never will."

You have to possess the desire to want to own a home. Your mind should be made up to not want to rent for the rest of your life. If being a homeowner is not a motivation, then you are wasting your time reading this book. I can give you every single step, but if you don't have the motivation to check out listings and comb through neighborhoods to find a home you deem is worth the investment, you will never be a home-owner.

Pre-qualification

This is the first active step to being a homeowner. Walk into your local mortgage company, credit union or bank and let them know you are looking to be a homeowner. Maybe your goal is to do it within the next year or two. Maybe you are in college and want to own a home by 25. Maybe you're engaged and want to purchase after the wedding. Everyone has their individual path and individual goals. Whatever your path is, one goal that is an absolute must is to be Lord of Your Land.

Go to a broker and ask to be pre-qualified. They will ask for a slew of information which may include, a copy of your driver's license, your social security card, two years' worth of W-2's or proof of income for two years. If you are just graduating from college, you will be asked for proof of employment in the form of a salary letter. They will also ask for recent bank statements and two recent pay stubs. Whatever they ask of you, supply it. If you only have $3 in the bank, give them a bank statement showing that you have $3.

Let them run your credit. You are allowed 7 credit pulls before your credit score is negatively affected. Stop using the excuse, "If they run my credit, it will hurt my score." This way of thinking is very idiotic. You are saying you want to buy a house, yet you're scared to let a mortgage broker run your credit so you can buy the house. Well, how do you expect to ever buy the house? How will you ever know what your credit looks like?

Stop being scared of what you may see. Let them see the bankruptcy, the old cell phone bill that was late, and the car loan where you were the co- signer for your sister and it got repossessed. It doesn't matter if you have a 400 credit score or if the screen reads 'N/A' which means non-applicable. The goal is if you get denied, they will tell you what steps to take to get your credit to a satisfactory score. No matter what the situation is, let them see it. You will see it as well. It will give a much better picture of what your checker board looks like.

The banker will let you know if you are approved and for what amount. If you cannot get the loan, they will tell you the reasons why, then you can find out what you need to address about those things so you can be approved. You work backwards to fix those things. This creates the perfect opportunity for you to ask the questions you need to ask.

Let's say you are approved for a home that's only $80,000, but the home you have in mind is $135,000. Find out what you have to do to qualify for the more expensive home. If they tell you, your credit score is a 690, and you have good income, yet you have only been at your job one year, then you know you have to work one more year before you can begin to look. I do not recommend that you pre-qualify online. Go into a place where you can sit face to face with a person you can touch and ask questions. If you don't like the first person you encounter, find another one. Remember, they work for you. Get someone who you feel really cares and has your best interest at heart.

I began working in the real estate industry as a loan officer making 30% commission as a 22year old to making 90% commission as the manager over two branches. I know and understand financing well. Some loan officers only care about their check today, while others care about building relationships with people over the course of a career. When I saw someone being qualified, I would put them on their path to ownership. Firstly, it helps them to fulfill their goal and secondly, the client will appreciate the loan officer who helps them meet their goal while referring them business.

No matter how bad you think your situation is, you can still find someone who is able to give you a checklist to get you on your way to purchasing that home. Don't get distracted by the music videos, the bling bling, parties and new cars. Keep homeownership a top priority on your list. Fight your fears…fight your excuses and begin your path to homeownership!

Credit

When looking at credit to apply for a mortgage, it's not always about a credit score. Yes, banks do look at your FICO score, usually the middle score. Banks can make up any rule that they want and at any time the guidelines for scores can change. Don't rely on the guidelines I'm giving you here, instead pay close attention to the guidelines the mortgage professional gives you.

There are a range of guidelines and not all are score-driven. You can have a 700 score that is based on only one credit card. Banks want to see multiple trade lines. Trade lines are actual credit activities that you have. If you only have one credit card, the bank will love the fact that you make $90,000 a year and have a score in the 700's, but you don't have enough accounts to prove to them that you can keep up regular payments.

So you will have to open up more lines of credit or ask someone to make you an authorized user on their cards. You can go get a small personal loan. Even after filing bankruptcy, there are programs out there to help you buy real estate just a year or two after filing.

"Credit is looking at the overall picture, not just the score."

I did a seminar for New Jersey City University on credit titled, *'How To Get A Perfect Credit Score'* which is on YouTube. Go to YouTube and type in the word 'credit', my video is on the first page. In the video, I go into detail about what to do to raise your score. I'll touch on it quickly here.

People will say it's a waste of time to get a secured credit card because of the interest the banks charge you, blah...blah...blah. The method which worked for me coming out of the hood, with a low income situation and no credit was as follows: I went into the bank, bought a CD that gained interest, and they gave me the money via a bank-secured loan. I then went to a second bank with that loan and got a secured credit card. I was able to pay down the secured loan and pay down the credit card. I didn't lose any money because the money I gave the bank for the CD, was given back to me in the form of a loan. Essentially, the money I walked in the bank with, I walked out with; just in a different form.

Yes, I had to pay high interest rates on my credit cards and high interest rates on my loan. People argued that I was just paying the banks' bills. Back to the idiotic thinking with excuses. If I pay 21% on a credit card on a third of the credit card's limit (never max out a card) in order for my credit score to boost 70, 90, 120 points in a year to establish the credit I need to accomplish my goal, I'm happy to pay the bank a couple dollars. I have effectively, legally established credit and I am that much closer to my goal.

Nothing in this world is really free. Go ahead and apply for store cards first. Anywhere you apply for credit is going to charge you interest. When the bank approves you for a mortgage, there is interest on your mortgage. To be quite honest, you pay more interest on your mortgage than you do the principal for the first 20 years of a 30-year mortgage. Car loans and leases are the same.

The people who talk down about using secured cards to improve credit are people who already have good credit or come from privilege. Maybe there is another way...this is what I know works. I receive countless emails from students of the Jay Morrison Academy who tell me this worked for them, they have tried this formula and their credit score escalated. So, I will continue to teach and preach this tried and true method. The whole premise is no excuses, just results. This is a way to acquire credit coming from no credit. Look at it like this, the banks see you as a risk, so you have to eliminate that risk by getting a secured line.

Income

Are you a wage earner employed by someone else? Are you an independent contractor or self-employed business owner where you pay yourself? Each type of employment will dictate exactly what the bank wants to see in terms of how many months or years of income you can prove. (is this what you were trying to say Jay, I wasn't sure?)

If you are a recent college graduate and have landed a job in the field that you studied, banks will give you credit towards the length of time you have been working on the job. You may be in a position where you simply don't make enough and have to get a second job. Sometimes it's just a matter of time, where you know what you have to do and you have to patiently wait it out. That doesn't mean the glass is half empty, it means you are on the path to put yourself closer to your goal. Work diligently and consistently towards becoming a homeowner.

Debt to Income

When your credit score is pulled, the mortgage professional will have a picture of your overall debt. The debt-to-income ratio is the amount of monthly debt you have compared to your monthly income. If you are making $3,000 a month and you owe $1,500 a month, you have a 50% debt- to-income ratio. Your debt ratio is 50% of your $3,000 income. Different banks will vary in their debt-to-income ratio requirements, so be mindful of that when talking to your mortgage broker.

Financial Freedom Fund (FFF)

Everyone should have an emergency or savings fund prior to purchasing their home, unless they display a higher tolerance for risk. I call it a Financial Freedom Fund, or FFF. Understand that my recommendation is for finances to be organized and well controlled. This is done by having a daily budget, a weekly budget, as well as a monthly budget. The overall goal is to get away from having to use the daily and weekly budget, focusing only on the monthly budget. To get a good grasp on the monthly budget, starting out with a daily and weekly budget is easier to handle.

The purpose of a budget is to see what you are spending versus what you are bringing in. Taking stock daily, weekly or monthly will show you where to make adjustments to increase positive cash flow while being smarter in your spending, thus lowering your expenses.

The second reason to do a budget is to multiply your monthly expenses by three (if you are more risky) or six (if you are more conservative), to provide a number to shoot for when aiming towards your FFF. You want three to six times your monthly expenses put up aside from the money you have set aside for purchasing a house.

Risky FFF

$2500 (monthly bills) x 3 (months) = $7500 in FFF

Conservative FFF

$2500 (monthly bills) x 6 (months) = $15,000 in FFF

As this is the first of several proactive steps towards your quest for financial freedom, I'd like to stress how important it is to make the necessary sacrifices to create this reserve FFF. Once you have calculated the figure to work towards work diligently. This may mean no vacation this year, forgoing the latest J's that hit the market, rocking last year's hot purses, less eating out and certainly no new vehicle.

Taking this step seriously by eliminating wasteful spending for a few months or maybe a year, will open the door figuratively and literally to your new home. Turning the key will be a much sweeter victory knowing how hard you worked for it. Cutting extra expenditures is important and should be the priority for every family, especially in pursuit of becoming Lord of Your Land, entrepreneurs and investors.

If you need to dip into your FFF for the down payment on your home, that is ok, as long as you have a perspective of how much you need saved based on your expenses. No matter what, you want to be in control of your spending.

For those who anticipate buying a multi-family home, keep in mind when doing your budget, there will be additional income coming in due to the rental units. This will adjust the way your monthly budget is set up after you are in the home and have rented the units, and think, "What if...", then they wake up at 40 and are still renting because they weren't brave enough to check out their financial picture.

JMA WealthDNA- DAILY BUDGET TRACKER

Week Of: | 20 |

Categories:

ay	ITEM	COST$	ITEM	COST$	ITEM	COST$	ITEM	COST$	ITEM	COST$	TOTAL
UN		$0.00		$0.00		$0.00		$0.00		$0.00	$0.00
ION											$0.00
UE											$0.00
ED											$0.00
HU											$0.00
RI											$0.00
AT											$0.00

TOTAL $0.00

31

JMA WealthDNA™ WEEKLY/ MONTHLY BUDGET TRACKER

Month: 20

Categories:

	WEEK 1	WEEK 2	WEEK 3	WEEK 4	WEEK 5	MONTH
INCOME						
Salary/ Revenue						$0.00
Interest Income						$0.00
Dividends						$0.00
Refunds/Reimbursements						$0.00
Other						$0.00
TOTAL	$0.00	$0.00	$0.00	$0.00	$0.00	$0.00
SAVINGS						$0.00
To Savings Account						$0.00
401K/ Other						$0.00
To Emergency Fund						$0.00
Charitable Donations						$0.00
Other						$0.00
TOTAL	$0.00	$0.00	$0.00	$0.00	$0.00	$0.00
HOME EXPENSES						$0.00
Mortgage/Rent						$0.00
Electricity						$0.00
Gas/Oil						$0.00
Water/Sewer/Trash						$0.00
Cable/Satellite						$0.00
Internet/ Phone						$0.00
Lawn/Garden						$0.00
Maintenance						$0.00
Other						$0.00
TOTAL	$0.00	$0.00	$0.00	$0.00	$0.00	$0.00
LIVING						$0.00
Groceries						$0.00
Personal Supplies						$0.00
Medical (Adult)						$0.00
Clothing						$0.00
Dry Cleaning						$0.00
Dining/Eating Out						$0.00
Babysitting						$0.00
Mobile Phone						$0.00
Other						$0.00
Medical (Child/ Children)						$0.00
Clothing (Child/ Children)						$0.00
School Tuition						$0.00
School Lunch						$0.00
School Supplies						$0.00
Other						$0.00
TOTAL	$0.00	$0.00	$0.00	$0.00	$0.00	$0.00
HEALTH						$0.00
Doctor/Dentist						$0.00
Medicine/Drugs						$0.00
Health Club Dues						$0.00
Emergency						$0.00
TOTAL	$0.00	$0.00	$0.00	$0.00	$0.00	$0.00
INSURANCE						$0.00
Auto						$0.00
Health						$0.00
Home/Rental						$0.00
Life						$0.00
Other						$0.00
TOTAL	$0.00	$0.00	$0.00	$0.00	$0.00	$0.00
EDUCATION						$0.00
Tuition						$0.00
Books/ Supplies						$0.00
Fees						$0.00
Other						$0.00
TOTAL	$0.00	$0.00	$0.00	$0.00	$0.00	$0.00
OBLIGATIONS						$0.00
Student Loan						$0.00
Other Loan						$0.00
Credit Card #1						$0.00
Credit Card #2						$0.00
Credit Card #3						$0.00
Alimony/Child Support						$0.00
Federal Taxes						$0.00
State/Local Taxes						$0.00
Bank Fees						$0.00
Other						$0.00
TOTAL	$0.00	$0.00	$0.00	$0.00	$0.00	$0.00
BUSINESS						$0.00
Deductible Expenses						$0.00
Non-Deductible Expenses						$0.00
Other						$0.00
TOTAL	$0.00	$0.00	$0.00	$0.00	$0.00	$0.00
ENTERTAINMENT						$0.00
Hobbies						$0.00
Events						$0.00
Travel						$0.00
Toys/Gadgets						$0.00
Other						$0.00
TOTAL	$0.00	$0.00	$0.00	$0.00	$0.00	$0.00
OTHER						$0.00
Other						$0.00
Other						$0.00
TOTAL	$0.00	$0.00	$0.00	$0.00	$0.00	$0.00
TOTAL	$0.00	$0.00	$0.00	$0.00	$0.00	$0.00

Monthly Total: $0.00

Now, you work with that mortgage broker and map out your game plan, your 'To Do List'. Put it on your refrigerator or somewhere prominent where you will see it on a regular basis. Make it the screen saver on your phone. It has to become one of the utmost priorities to conquer. It may take 1, 2 or 3 years. Do what you have to do to put yourself in the position to do what you came to do, which is to be Lord of Your Land. Tell your friends, spouse, significant other, kids and parents what you are trying to accomplish so they will hold you responsible. Half of the fight is knowing where you stand. I didn't get qualified the first time I went in, but I made sure that every kink was ironed out so I could purchase my first home by 25 years old.

Financing Options

FHA

The Fair Housing Administration is a government-backed insurance for homes. The FHA does not give the loans; however, it provides the guidelines for loans. It was created to permit more flexibility for qualifying home buyers. This is done partly by allowing for very low down payments.

Guidelines can change at any time, so it is important to get in touch with a mortgage professional to find out where you fit. FHA homes are meant to be owner-occupied, not purchased as an investment.

The credit guidelines are lenient. You are allowed to have your down payment paid by a family member as a gift, in addition to getting the seller to pay the closing costs. That means you would have to pay no money down on an FHA house. However, you will have to pay private mortgage insurance (PMI).

PMI is like an extra payment on top of your mortgage payment. There is homeowner's insurance, taxes, mortgage payment which is principal and interest, as well as PMI. Its purpose is to protect the lender against losses should the borrower default. With conventional loans, there is no need to pay PMI, as long as you put down 20% or more as your down payment, therefore the mortgage payment will be lower.

203k

This is a renovation loan available through FHA where they will give you a loan based on the post-renovation value of the home. An inspector will come out to gauge how much the property will be worth if certain improvements are made. Based on that value, they will loan money to renovate in phases.

There are guidelines that dictate the type of acceptable contractors. I highly suggest you deal with a mortgage professional who is experienced in 203k loans, not an inexperienced person. They are not hard loans to obtain, but using someone who is well versed in the 203k loans will alleviate potential headaches. Same thing with the Realtor and contractor you use. Get a team who all have had experience dealing with this specific type of loan.

VA

They are similar to FHA loans, but are specifically, for veterans. Look up guidelines to make yourself familiar with them. Sadly, there are a lot of veterans who do not take advantage of this loan. Two major perks are $0 down payment and no PMI required.

Conventional Financing

This form of funding is where banks and brokers have programs outside of FHA or VA loans. This option will have competitive rates and their own guidelines as another way to be able to afford a home.

Seller Financing

You may get lucky enough to find a house that you like and the seller owns the house free and clear. There is no mortgage. The seller may be willing to let you purchase the property, occupy the property, and have contractual rights to the property while you pay the mortgage payment directly to the seller based on whatever terms you agree upon. I wholeheartedly suggest you only do this with an attorney. Do not be   frugal (do be frugal in your everyday spending) and try to negotiate this type of transaction yourself. Pay for an attorney to advise you. In this situation, the seller is happy making interest on the property, similar to rent. You are the owner unless you default on the property.

Leasing With the Option To Buy

You have found the property that you want to buy, but are unable to qualify right away. You move in and pay rent to the seller with the understanding that those payments will be applied to the down payment or to the principal. These agreements should be drawn up by your attorney for the length of time that is decided by you and the seller.

Private Financing/Hard Money

Private financing is usually reserved for investors, not first time homeowners. Private lenders will charge more fees up front with higher interest rates. Instead of having an interest rate of 6%, private lenders will charge upwards of 18%.

Homes which are going to be bought, renovated and sold immediately are more ideal for this type of loan. You are paying more for the loan, but there is more profit to be made so you would not mind paying more as long as you can flip it quickly to make a profit. This route is not recommended for first time homeowners, I just wanted to touch on it.

Three Under-utilized Strategies

Tap Into Your Income

Most banks, including when qualifying for an FHA loan, will allow you to use Section 8, disability vouchers, government checks, veteran checks and sometimes even alimony and child support towards your income during the purchase of a home. It is very important that you itemize these sources of income, if you have them. Using them will increase your purchasing power.

Future Rental Credit

Most banks will give you future rental credit. This means if you are buying a 2, 3 or 4unit home, that will be owner-occupied, the bank gives you credit for the additional units that will be rented out. For example, Keep in mind, if you are buying a multi-family home, the banks will give you credit for the projected future rental income. For example, if you are purchasing a 3unit property, the first unit is yours to live in, however you can claim between 85-95% credit for projected future rental income. This credit will be added to your existing income to make you a stronger candidate to become a homeowner. Say you are working at a fast food joint only making $20,000 annually, looking to purchase a 4unit property. You plan on renting out the other 3 units at

$1,000 per month which gives you an additional $3,000 income per month. The bank will credit 85-95% of that $3,000 to your existing monthly income. That is an additional $2,550 to $2,850 added income each month or $30,600 to $34,200 annually!

Use More Co-Borrowers

In the African-American community, this is something that is really not taken advantage of. Banks will allow you to use more than one co- borrower on an owner-occupied mortgage loan. Let me paint a picture. You work at Wal-Mart, grandma has a social security voucher and you need her income, your cousin works at Burger King and you need his income, both of them can be on the loan with you for one property.

Living with other people is a sacrifice many people don't want to make to be Lord of their Land-- not realizing that land and homeownership are one of the biggest wealth-making tools in America. So, if income, credit or savings is an issue and you cannot get qualified for a home, leverage the income, credit and savings of others.

Proof of Funds, Preapproval and Prequalification (PPP)

This acronym represents yet another stage of the finance game. You have to be able to prove to a bank that you have the money or financing in place to purchase their home. A bank will ask for proof of funds if you are purchasing a home traditionally, as a foreclosure or a short sale, and a homeowner will ask for it if you are purchasing a For Sale by Owner (FSBO). PPP can be shown in cash, a certified letter from your Certified Public Accountant (CPA), a notarized or certified letter from the attorney who handles your accounts (i.e. trusts), or a bank, mortgage company or broker who has pre-qualified you.

The difference between a prequalification letter and a preapproval is that the latter is a softer overview of your finances and credit, not necessarily guaranteeing you have been qualified. Prequalification is the next step up from pre-approval where the bank digs a little deeper into your background and actually sends an application to their underwriters where they review for compliance and issue final loan approval, once certain conditions have been met. This list of conditions, also known as stipulations or "STIPS" outlines what else is needed before they are able to issue the final loan approval. Keep in mind your Realtor or mortgage broker will help you to complete the STIPS because they don't get paid unless the transaction closes. Use your team to clear the list.

P – Proof of funds – bank statement, 401K statement or any of the aforementioned letters.

P – Pre-approval – is enough to get you shopping for a home, but more hard evidence needs to be shown.

P – Prequalification – allows you to walk into your home search confident that you can afford it.

Buyers' Market vs. Sellers' Market

When is the best time to buy? When everybody is trying to sell! Why? Because there are more sellers on the market which means they have to lower their price to compete with each other. This brings in the law of supply and demand. If there are limited buyers (demand) with an abundance of houses to choose from (supply), the sellers must decrease their price in order to move their properties. Do not buy when everyone else is buying because sellers know they can demand more than the appraised value -- as a potential buyer will be willing to pay more, in order to compete with other potential buyers for the same property. You should never pay more for a property than it is worth! In teaching you when to buy, how to build a team, and understanding the rules of engagement in real estate to become Lord of Your Land, we empower more astute, well informed and educated buyers in their quest to build wealth. As we all know, real estate is the cornerstone to building wealth.

Step 2
Building Your Team

Whether approved or denied, please ensure you ask the broker or banker for the blueprint outlining your next steps. If approved, you are now in a position to start looking to purchase. There are some key players who you are going to need on your team. Conversely, every real estate agent is not a Realtor. A Realtor is a real estate agent who is part of a Real Estate Association.

A good real estate agent will let you know that you need a team. Being that I am one, you will be fully prepared to walk into homeownership. This book was written with a dual purpose in mind. One was to ensure anyone who reads it will be well-equipped to be Lord of Their Land and secondly, it eliminates any of the guess work one may have about the process. After the qualification, you have the option to stick with the lender, also called a mortgage broker who qualified you or not. There is no contract that says you have to be financed by that particular person or entity. If they have done a good job by you and you like the energy, then by all means remain with them. On the contrary, if they have changed jobs or if things between you just didn't seem to quite gel, then move on to find someone you are comfortable with. Remember, all of these people work for you.

This would be a great place to start looking for a Realtor. Ask your lender, friends or family members for a referral to a good Realtor or real estate agent because you will need one. You want to ensure your real estate agent and your mortgage broker are licensed. You want to also hire a real estate attorney. Now keep in mind, all of the people you are coming into contact with will have referrals for the other members you will need on your team.

You will need a property inspector. You do not have to have your property inspected, but being that you're new to home purchasing, it is the wise move to make. Your loan officer will likely refer you to a title agent or closing agent. This person is responsible for ensuring the property is free and clear (free from Title defects to include recorded liens, permits, judgments, etc.) for you to own.

ave an attorney and

ecommend you do.

rs to work on the

here are repairs that

can count on for

you obtain home-

protects the bank's

, they want to know

if something goes

al. I bought a house

to get homeowners

insurance simply because there was no bank enforcing it. I

went away for the weekend and received a call while I was

away. As fate would have it, the house caught fire. I was sick

to my stomach thinking about the damage I was going to

walk back into. Thankfully, nobody was injured, but there

was so much damage to the house that it ended up being a total loss.

"A perk to owning property…not only do you own the dwelling, the land it sits on, and the mineral rights to what's below the surface, but you also own rights to the air above it."

If you find gold, oil, granite, coal or any natural resource of value, it is yours to develop and sell. You also have air rights which means if you want to build up, you can do so. Yep, that's right! You own the air above your land too! The area above your home cannot be developed without your consent. Air rights are big in cities like New York. The land is tight, so they build up, not out. Homeowners sell air rights to provide space for sky scrapers and big buildings to be erected.

You're The Boss

You are looking for your first home and you're very intimidated. You encounter a real estate agent who has been there for 13 years and is quite experienced. You feel like that person should be in charge, they should be leading the way. But remember, your real estate agent, your mortgage professional, your contractor, all these people work...for...you! They are consultants who will advise you, offer you best practices, they can tell you about their experiences or what other clients have done and even what they recommend. You call all the shots. You make the final decision; you are the boss!

Do not let yourself get into a situation that you are not comfortable with. If your instincts are telling you something isn't right, double and triple check the situation. If the person is talking fast and you don't understand, slow them down. You don't have to pretend to be a know-it-all. You are the bread winner of that project, if you don't close on the house and sign on the dotted line, no one gets paid. Understand the dynamics of what is at play. You are the lord of the transaction.

In my previous experiences, I trusted my lawyers and Realtors because they had so much more experience than I did. I didn't double check them, I let them talk fast and it ended up costing me. A personal example of me not being lord of my transaction cost me almost $250,000.

After establishing my credit, I set out to buy my first property. I put the house under contract and called an inspector out. Tenants were already there which would have brought me $2,000 a month profit in rental income. The inspection came back saying a joint beam was bent in the basement. My agent told me to terminate the contract because he thought the beam issue was too severe and would be a headache in the future. I listened. I didn't do any research, didn't do any due diligence, didn't seek a second opinion. I just listened to my Realtor and let him be lord of the transaction.

I cancelled the transaction. Two years later, that same property sold for $390,000…when I had it under contract, it was only $189,000! I missed out on $200,000 in profits, plus two years of rental income. What I learned down the road is that properties are big, heavy buildings sitting on a foundation. Those beams shift as a part of earth moving, along with gravity taking its toll. It's a normal occurrence. It was in no way as dramatic as my Realtor made it seem.

I could have simply gone to buy a jack from a home improvement store to jack the house up and bring support. The jack would have cost about $3,000 that the seller would have paid for after the inspection and the situation would have been rectified. That lack of knowledge by my Realtor and me not doing my due diligence as a home buyer cost me a few hundred grands. Not to mention it was set up for Section 8 rent which is guaranteed income. I really missed out on a great transaction for me and what could have been a great legacy builder for my family.

My point in telling you this is to show that it is okay to get a second opinion. Don't worry about offending your Realtor or your mortgage broker. If you feel your mortgage broker isn't giving you a good deal because you don't like the interest rate, down payment or programs that are being offered to you, go somewhere else.

How to Find Your Team?

The route that I use is to interview three people in each position. This allows me to gauge three different systems, three different personalities and gives a good perspective on what's right and what's wrong. You are able to get price points and they will compete against each other. You can check out the information they are giving you by bouncing it off of the others.

Interviewing three people can happen independently or through referrals. Going the independent route, you are finding them on your own, looking up your own references using Facebook, Google or any other myriad of resources.

Using referrals requires you go through other professionals, so it depends on how confident you are in their professional relationships and abilities.

What Role Your Team Plays

Loan Officers prequalify or qualify you and submit your loan to the bank(s) that will inevitably finance your transaction. They will be working with you, your agent, your attorney and everyone else on your team to keep the transaction funded and get it closed. Whatever information the bank needs to secure   your loan will come through this person. This key player is responsible for making sure the transaction is funded. They may have to adjust your preapproval based on the property you decide on.

Say you have been preapproved for a home that is $180,000 and you find a home for $150,000, but you decide to lowball the offer and go in at

$140,000. You don't want to show a preapproval letter with $180,000 on it. The seller will be offended that you are lowballing them when it's obvious that you can afford the asking price.

On the other side of that coin, you may find a home for $190,000 and have to go back to find out what you can do to get the preapproval raised.

"What can go wrong, will go wrong."

There are all kinds of things that could arise during the course of buying a home. There could be issues with title, other documents, or something could show on your credit that you thought was previously handled. Don't get frustrated. Be persistent and get the transaction done.

Real estate professionals are responsible for gathering details from you to help find a house that meets most, if not all, of your requirements in a realistic price range and in the area that you want. A good agent will ask you a lot of questions to find out what your needs are. The more specific your wants and needs are in the beginning, the less time, energy and frustration you will encounter during the "viewing" properties process.

Simply saying you want a single family ranch is too vague and not   specific enough. There are many   features that make a home desirable to a prospective buyer. Do you want a pool? Do you want the pool to be above ground or below ground? Do you want a driveway? How many bedrooms? How many bathrooms? Does the garage have to be attached? Do you want a garage for one car, two cars or three? Is there anyone in the home with special needs? Is there anyone elderly in the home who has trouble getting around or is in a wheelchair? What kind of kitchen do you want? Does a "man cave" matter to you? Do you want a corner lot? Do you want a gated community? Do you need a fence? There are so many details that, if gathered upfront, make the Realtor's life easier which will make your life easier, getting you to your goal faster.

The agent will also hold your hand and fight for you tooth and nail to get you to the closing table so they can be paid. The Realtor gets paid by the seller when the transaction closes, not by you, the buyer. Getting to the closing includes making sure you have   homeowner's insurance, helping you get into the house, going back and forth to the property to have your inspection done, helping to rectify any issues found and so on.

Attorney

This team member will ensure your contract and any required amendments to the contract are complete, accurate and written with your best interest in mind. He or she will be the driver of the transaction from a legal perspective. The attorney is responsible for overseeing the transaction, ensuring it takes place in a timely manner, and making sure you receive the fixtures noted in the contract, etc.

There are two types of fixture, permanent and removable. There could be chandeliers and blinds, for example, that you think you are getting and the seller intends to take them. If you can remove the fixture with a screwdriver, it is not considered a permanent fixture. If your attorney and real estate agent aren't doing their jobs, you could put a contract on a home and think you are getting beautiful ceiling fans in every room, but since that is not in the contract, the seller can strip them from the home – legally. The same with appliances, pool tables, furniture or anything you see when viewing the home and want to keep, those items must be negotiated in the contract at some point before closing.

Inspector

This person will make sure your home is thoroughly inspected.

Title Agent

Someone will have to do title searches on the property to make sure it is free and clear of any title defects and ensure you are the true legal owner upon closing.

Benefits of In-House Relations vs. Bringing Your Own Team

If you do decide to go with referrals from working professionals, they will more than likely refer you to people who they have worked with in the past. You have to be careful that you are getting a referral based on quality and not friendship or any other kind of business relationship.

They may refer you to someone they have a business relationship with because there is some sort of unethical or illegal kickback in it for them. They could have a tag team plan, "If I send you somebody, you send me somebody." They could be looking out for their best interests as opposed to yours. You want referrals based on who they think is the best person for you, your situation and your personality.

Don't feel obligated to go with whom they refer. That person may not work out for you, you may not see eye to eye or you may feel that they don't have the expertise you need. Double check those referrals and be sure you are comfortable with them. Understand that close relationships can work out well, however, "Caveat Emptor," a Latin term, meaning - Buyer beware!

"Remember you are the lord of the transaction and you make the final call. "

How to Decide On Your Team
Professionalism and Integrity

In interviewing potential team members, you want to know their experience and how long they have been in the business. You are looking for true professionalism and integrity. Professionalism first, then integrity, and then experience. Someone could have 20 years of experience and be lackadaisical when   compared to someone who has been in the industry for 3 years, but who is young, eager and hungry to do a great job.

A true professional may not have all the answers, but they will admit they don't before doing their best to find out what you want to know. You would rather them be honest than to act like a know-it-all or someone who tells you lies.

You want someone with integrity who does what they say they are going to do. If they say they are going to call at 6, they need to call you at 6, and they should not stand you up for a showing; those types of things.

Enthusiasm. You want someone who is hungry and excited, because that person is going to work hard for you. Sometimes people automatically go with someone who is older and more experienced. Don't underestimate someone who is younger who has great mentors with a plethora of experience.

Chemistry. This is a person who you are going to be spending a great deal of time with. Lots of talking on the phone, emails, they will be handling business on your behalf and you want to make sure that you mesh well together.

Step 3
House Shopping

How to Pick Your First House?

You want to be very specific in what you are looking for so your agent can do a good job of helping you find properties. The main thing is discovering the attributes in a home that actually matter to you, keeping in mind that your dream home may be another 10 years away. And that is okay! You can still have what reasonably satisfies your needs today.

What's important is that you stop wasting money in rent, and start gaining appreciation in equity and awareness as the Lord of Your Land. A lot of time we aim to get our dream home today and that is just not realistic. Instead, we will go rent a condo or a townhouse and it gives us the "look" that we want, and it's so sexy, but we don't even own it!

The train of thought needs to change to appreciating what you can get, what you can own, even if it is not as big as you want or in the exact area. If you can walk into your dream home on the first try, good for you. If not, like the rest of us, focus on making a great first step getting into homeownership, knowing the house is setting you up to get the dream home in the future.

Your Realtor will find several listings that meet your requirements and more than likely send them to you in an email. Then you will get together to discuss what was sent. You go out and look at houses in person, testing the market. When you find a home that makes you feel all warm and fuzzy and fits your criteria, you put a contract on it. Once you let your Realtor know 'this is the one', he or she and your attorney will get to the nitty gritty of the contractual obligations. If the contract is accepted, you submit it to your mortgage officer so they can submit it to the banks and begin the process of buying your home. Then you may commence the home inspection and the due process of closing on the house.

Depending on what part of the country you are in, there are different types of homes that are more popular than others. There are pros and cons to each. Here is a list of the categories of homes.

Trailer Home

Popular in rural areas, ranging from single to triple wide, however there is no foundation and they can easily be moved. The banks require a special type of financing for that called Certified Trailer Home Financing. There is also a title needed likened to a car title because they can be hitched and pulled by vehicles.

Condo

Your rights are limited because of the associations that govern condos. You do not have rights to the air property and common spaces are shared. You do own space within the condominium. Condos are usually cheaper because of the shared space. Association fees take care of maintenance issues that may arise, including lawn care. You have access to pools, gyms and cook out areas. There is a special homeowner's insurance because you are insuring only the belongings within your walls, not the whole condo building.

Townhouse

A collection of property similar to a condo, but has a distinguished entrance and many times offers some sort of a yard or patio.

Row Home

Similar to how a townhome is set up, but without the governing association. They appear to be single family homes that are attached on both sides. When homes are separated by a minimum of 1 foot, they are no longer considered row homes because they are not physically sharing a wall.

Single Family

Many different types, one dwelling, a single unit on a property. You own the property, the land that surrounds it, the ground below it and the air above it. There are no other units on the property. Comes with the advantage of multiple tax benefits.

Multi Family

Comprised of 1 to 4 units, as anything over 4 is considered commercial property. Can purchase as an owner-occupied unit if you are going to live in one of the units. The point to buying this type is to rent the other units for rental income. Tax benefits on the rental units.

Rehabs & New Construction

Rehabilitation properties are those that need renovations and can be any home from a trailer home to a multi-family. You will need to secure a contracting team to bring together the vision for how you want your home to look. This could be as simple as renovating a bathroom or as complicated as knocking down walls and making additions.

New construction can be configured different ways. You can purchase a lot of land and get financing to build on the land which is called stick build – a traditional building, where a foundation is put down and the home is built up. A developer will use their own specs or build the home to meet your specifications as in a custom built home. This process can take anywhere from 6 months on.

Modular or pre-fab build describes a home built in a factory or warehouse, then brought to the property and placed on the foundation by cranes in phases. The home is able to be built quicker because it is done in a facility, which is a controlled weather environment.

Knock down – a situation where there is a home on land, but the buyer is only interested in the land with plans to buy the home and tear it down to build an entirely brand new home. They literally come in with a bulldozer, knocking down the entire house, rebuilding the foundation and starting completely over.

How to Negotiate Your Offer?

"In negotiations, whoever cares the least, has the most power."

This must be understood going into the transaction. You could find the house of your dreams with an indoor pool, an elevator, cascading stairway in the perfect school district and at your price point. In your mind, there is no way you could have found a better house, but the seller has four houses just like it and doesn't care if you buy this house or not. In this negotiation, the seller is going to be the most powerful and they can toy with you because you care more.

Flipping the coin, the seller could be motivated because they just got a divorce or lost a job and don't want to lose the property because they can no longer afford it. You have found six properties you are looking at, which gives you the power because you are not pressed to buy that particular house. In some cases, neither party really cares or both parties do care, but usually one will care much more than the other. The goal is for the property to exchange hands in a fair sale where there is no robbery.

You must be aware of the type of market it is, meaning is it a buyers' market or sellers' market? Buyers' market means there are more homes for sale than buyers, giving buyers leverage. During the recent meltdown, there were more buyers than there were homes to buy, so the sellers had the upper hand indicating it was a sellers' market. There was a great demand for houses, but not enough to supply all those who were in the market to buy.

When negotiating on property, I don't believe in playing games. Some people get caught up in the fun of negotiating, going back and forth. I am a firm believer in aggressive negotiating. If you know you need to move quickly, you should be less aggressive in your negotiating. You should not low ball an offer, sending the seller a figure that may be mutually agreeable knowing that you want the transaction to progress quickly.

Ask yourself this question: If my offer gets rejected and the house goes under contract to another buyer, would I be upset that I lost the house? If the answer is yes, you would be upset having played around and someone else got the property, then make your best offer on the property. It does not mean that you have to offer the full asking amount, but something that would be appealing to the seller. If you are not in a rush, you just want a great deal and you see something you can establish equity in, i.e. learning that a property is valued at more than the asking price, start with an offer that's insulting. If you feel like it will make the seller's face turn red or purple, put it in.

Equity is the amount of value over your mortgage. The value of the house has to be less than (Jay is this what you meant to say here regarding wanting value to be less than the purchase price?) the purchase price in this instance. Let's say the purchase price is $100,000, but you are putting at least 3.5% down, so your loan amount will be $96,500. Your purchase price and loan amount will almost always be two different figures.

Sometimes you get lucky and there's already a deal there. The home has equity built into it and the asking price has been discounted, just make a full price offer. Your agent will be able to tell you that. I teach this formula to all my students in the Jay Morrison Academy. A home that is worth 65% of the after-repair value is a very good deal. For instance, you have a house that is worth $100,000 and you can buy and renovate that house for $65,000. Anything at 65% is a very good deal in a home buyer's or investor's world. If you find a home like this, run with it! Hug it! Love it! And be on your merry way. 70-75% is still good, but 65% is a steal.

It is a known practice to ask for the seller to pay closing costs, called a seller's concession/ contributions or seller's assist. In this case, the seller will bump up the selling price on the home, which your bank will cover in financing, to prevent you from coming out of pocket with closing costs of 3-6%. They will instead be factored into the loan.

The Inspection Process

Once you get a property under contract, different states have varying procedures as far as how they handle the next steps. Your attorney or legal staff will walk you through it.

Most places will give you a certain length of time for a contract review, which gives you time to look more closely at the transaction to see if there is anything else you want to add or ask for. This time allows for negotiations to take place, on both sides, if applicable.

The contract allows the buyer to have time to get an inspection of the property and based upon the results of the inspection either choose to move forward with the transaction or not. Even in an inspection on a brand new house, something will probably show that can be improved because the inspections are so detailed. They cover termites, mold, the ceiling, appliances, foundational and structural aspects of the house... basically every nook and cranny of the house.

The cost of a typical inspection will range between $500 and $1,000. The inspector works with the buyer and their purpose is to uncover potential problems with the house that you should be aware of before buying. If you decide to purchase the home from a private seller, a friend or family member of yours who is selling the home without necessarily putting it on the market, you may choose to forgo the inspection. You may think the house looks good to you, feel confident it was taken care of very well and feel comfortable buying the house with no inspection.

Sellers may put clauses in the contract or with the listing indicating the house is being sold "as is," which is essentially saying, you are welcome to get an inspection, but don't come back with any repairs, because you are buying it in the condition that it is in. If you go through with an inspection, you want to have a contingency in the contract stating that in order for you to move forward with the transaction, there are some issues/ repairs that need to be addressed.

You may request that the seller credit you the amount necessary to repair whatever issue(s) arose that are not up to your standard in the selling costs. Or, after bringing up issues that are pertinent to you, the seller may disagree, not wanting to fix them and you can walk away from the transaction or the seller may compromise by giving you credit at closing.

Another option is to have the seller fix the issue(s) themselves and have the home re- inspected.

Banks used to have no problem crediting buyers with money at closing to fix repairs after the home has been purchased, however in recent times, they prefer the issues are fixed by the seller or agreed upon prior to getting to the closing table. Banks simply aren't as lenient in giving away that money. The seller or bank may decrease the selling price of the home so you can put that money into making the repairs. With this option, resolving the problem doesn't affect their pockets as much as it would affect yours.

Say the repairs are estimated at $3,000 and the selling price is decreased by that much, your mortgage only goes down about $17 a month over a 30year term. However, if those issues are something you want repaired immediately, that means you would have to spend that $3,000 immediately. Your options regarding the findings of an inspection are:

A. Move Forward

B. Walk Away

C. Compromise on the Issues

D. Seller Drops Purchase Price

Your preference as a buyer is have the seller fix it or work with your bank to credit you that money after closing to fix it. Most banks will require you to have an inspection prior to them approving the loan on the house. It is also good to note that inspectors won't charge for a re- inspection; if they do, that can also be negotiated in the selling cost.

Understanding Your Appraisal

After the inspection has been agreed upon and you're ready to move forward with the transaction, the bank is going to want to know that the property is worth the money they are loaning you to pay for it. If you opt to pay in cash, you should still want an appraisal for the same reason. You want to know that something is actually worth what you are going to be paying for it. An appraisal for a single family home in most markets will run about $375.

The gist of an appraisal is the appraiser finds three properties within one square mile that are similar to the property you are interested in. They are looking for the same bedroom and bathroom count, same square footage, garages, in addition to other household specs that have been sold within the last 3-6 months. They will come up with a comparative analysis of the property. The appraisal amount should be equal to what the selling price is or greater.

If the appraisal shows the property to be of a lesser value, then you have the option to walk away from the transaction or negotiate with the seller to lower the price. The bank will only loan you what the appraisal says the house is worth. In this case, where the appraisal came back less, if the seller won't budge to bring the price down, you will have to pay the difference in cash. Say the house is $200,000 and the appraisal says the home is worth $185,000. If you still want the house, you will have to come up with the extra $15,000 in addition to whatever cash you were putting as a down payment and/or closing costs. Your options are:

A. Pay More

B. Kill the transaction

C. Negotiate the Price

Step 4
Getting to the Closing Table

You accepted the call for homeownership, then executed the necessary steps. You fought the fear and actually got prequalified. No matter how long it took, you made the necessary steps to go from prequalification to qualification.

You built a team and went house shopping, you found the house that spoke to you. Maybe it was the house of your dreams, a great property as an investor or a house in the right school district for your children. Now you have had the inspection and negotiated the cost, the appraisal has led to a re- negotiation and the seller budged on the price.

The mortgage company has pushed your loan from underwriters to processors while your agent has been there with you the whole time keeping you in the loop. The bank has contacted your agent and notified them that the close date has been pushed back and the seller's bank wants a loan commitment. More credentials need to be verified, your social security number, a copy of your driver's license, pay stubs and bank statements. You have to make sure you have homeowners' insurance for the home you are about to purchase, as well as making sure your taxes are   paid up to date. The bank will be making sure the title is clear, scouring through records to ensure there are no liens or encumbrances on the property.

If the title shows what is called a crabby title, the seller has to rectify those things before selling the home to you. They will have to pay outright to make the title free and   clear.   If something does show up, they will hold a portion of the seller's money in escrow and still move forward with the transaction. Say a lien for $30,000 pops up in the search for which the seller believes they have already satisfied the terms of the lien, the bank will go through with the sale and hold $30,000 in escrow until the seller can prove it has been taken care of.

That amount is just in case it cannot be proven and that amount is needed to lift the lien.

Re-Negotiations & Amendments

If there is anything that doesn't look right, isn't agreeable or is not what you expected, these things should be brought up to your attorney, real estate agent or a member of your real estate team. The mortgage interest rate may suddenly jump or something could stand out as being inconsistent with what you expect. If something seems to have been hidden in the contract or there are parts that were not fully explained to you, always bring these concerns up and have them evaluated.

"Any issues should be addressed prior, NOT at the closing table."

Clear too close! This is music to every buyer's ears, every seller's ears, every mortgage broker and Realtor's ears. That means the transaction is good to go and all STIPS have been met.

Approaching the Closing Table

The title agent, an attorney brought in by the bank, and your real estate agent will be at the table. They don't get paid until the transaction goes through. You get a closing date and are excitedly ready to move in. Understand a lot of things are at play by this point and the closing date can get pushed around. If the date is set for a Friday and the bank doesn't get the wire to the mortgage company to pay the seller by 3:00 p.m., nobody gets paid. This is real money here! We are talking hundreds of thousands of dollars. Expect push backs and it's okay, because this is part of the business. But now, you have to wait another week or so to do the closing.

Make sure you do a walk through. Have a checklist of things that should have been repaired, replace d   or changed. Any questions or specifications you have about how the home works, write them down and ask the seller while you still have access to him/her. You want to be able to get as much information as you can about being the owner of that house. Is there a certain way to close the pantry door? Be sure to inquire about the location of the furnace or air conditioner and if there are any keys needed to access these.

Whatever changes you want made to the house, have those vendors prepared and ready to go with your closing date. Locksmiths and security companies should be identified during this time so you are not scrambling after closing trying to find and compare rates for these services.

Day of Closing

Walk in with a good attitude and a positive mindset, having thanked God that morning for the opportunity to own a home. At the closing, once again you have to prove you are who you say you are. That requires a driver's license and often times a social security card. You are going to sign a mountain of documents...don't be scared. Then you are given the keys to the property. Any issues that you had with the property should be corrected by this point. Anything that was agreed upon to get the home to the condition that you want should be satisfied.

You have to make sure the property is in the condition you expect it to be based on the construction and inspection. That means checking the property to make sure the seller didn't take anything from the home that they were not supposed to take or strip and damage the home in any way. If that happens, the transaction should be paused or frozen because you want it restored to the condition you expected it to be in.

The title will be handed to you. You hand over any money, most likely in the form of a cashier's check, get your keys and shake hands. If there is any money you are owed for repairs or credited back to you, it will be given at that time. Most states require that a security deposit be put into an interest-bearing account, which will be handed back over to you. You will also receive a form that has all the fees listed out, line by line. You walk out of the office a brand new homeowner and you take possession of the property on that day! Congratulations!

You also want to make sure that you receive any codes that will help you transition into the home easier, for example, garage door openers or passcodes and gate or security codes. An excellent new homeowner practice is to change the locks to have a fresh start and alleviate your mind from the concern that someone else could have a key to your home; especially if the home is not a brand new home. If it is a brand new home, the locks may not be of good quality, at which time you would also want to change them out.

The mortgage is a contract with the bank saying that you will make good on the loan, paying a certain amount every month for the next 15 to 40 years to satisfy the terms of the loan. If you default, or don't make good on the loan, the bank is allowed to foreclose on the property.

Definitely consider getting a home warranty, especially one that covers major appliances. Do the research on what a home warranty can do for you? Depending upon the condition of the major appliances, which you will be aware of during the inspection, repairs and replacement on those things can be very expensive. It is not unreasonable to ask for the seller to replace an air condition unit that is on its last leg.

Step 5
Post-Closing Practices
& Strategies

Congratulations! You did it. After months of putting to good use all of the information, advice, wisdom, and suggestions well-wishers have imparted...

YOU DID IT!

You purchased your first home. Hard work, a few sacrifices and an awesome team of professionals all made it happen. Although the road has had a few potholes, you actually made it. Now for the part not many discuss: what happens after closing. You have signed your loan documents and deed; you have your keys...now what?

Here are a few valuable tips you may want to consider:

If you have the option, take a day or two to properly organize and facilitate your move. You will feel much less anxiety than if you rush and are not properly prepared for what lies ahead.

Moving

1. If you don't already have one, arrange for a security company to meet you for an alarm system installation IMMEDIATELY after closing. In many cases, the neighbors and contractors are aware that the property has been vacant and may have new appliances, etc. Avoid any mishaps by installing the alarm before taking your personal effects into your home.

2. Your mortgage company requires certain types of insurance on the loan and the structure of your home. What you may or may not have been advised to do is make certain you have adequate insurance on the contents of your home. Your personal belongings are about to enter the property and you want to avoid potential loss as a result of damage or theft throughout the move.

3. Contact all of the necessary utility companies (gas, electric, water, cable, internet, etc.). Have the accounts transferred to your new address, or into your name if they are already on. In a perfect world, we can schedule all these installations simultaneously so that all can be done and out of the way. Also, remember the alarm will require electricity.

4. Locate a reputable mover. In these days of being fiscally responsible, we all want a bargain. Craigslist, Penny Saver, the bulletin board at the grocery or hardware store all have flyers and posts advertising moving services.

PLEASE BEWARE. Everyone that is capable of performing a task isn't necessarily qualified to perform it. Make certain your mover is insured, bonded and licensed by the jurisdiction you live in. In the absolute worst case scenario; if there is an accident, you can be reimbursed or compensated through the company's insurance. Also, check several references yourself. Not all internet reviews are authentic. Ask for a customer if possible and talk to them yourself. Call them! Ask specific questions about the service, the personnel, punctuality and other specifics regarding their experience. Keep in mind these people are about to have access to all of your personal belongings. Not doing your due diligence could be opening your home for someone who is a potential thief or even worse, a burglar.

5. Introduce yourself to your neighbors. That "nosey" neighbor we all try to avoid can be the same one who accepts a package for you that you really needed, or better still, deters someone from trespassing on what was once the neighborhood vacant house.

6. If possible, keep a reserve fund of a few hundred dollars for the "just in case" scenario. You would be surprised at the things that come up in a new home that need to be taken care of right away; light bulbs, batteries, doorstops, bug spray, you get the drift. If you depleted all your funds at closing, don't be too proud to tell a friend or family member a Visa gift card would be a helpful housewarming gift.

7. A home warranty is a MUST HAVE! As a Realtor, I personally give all of my clients a one-year home warranty as a closing gift. This will protect you from out of pocket repair expenses in your new home. A traditional home warranty will cover repairs to some structural issues, as well as plumbing, roofing, and even appliances and mechanical (hot water heater, furnace, etc.). It never hurts to ask for it at closing, but if you are

not able to have it gifted to you, you can purchase one for about $400 per year. Well worth the investment. It can save you thousands.

8. Keep a record of any malfunctions or repair issues that arise in the first 60-90 days. If you have a good real estate agent and they maintain good relationships, they may very well be able to have the seller make those repairs to show good intentions.

Maintaining Your Property

All leases and security deposits will be put into your name. If you are purchasing a property that has tenants, your lawyer and real estate team will produce eviction notices giving the time to move out of the property. When I purchase a property that has tenants, I will go to the property to announce myself not as the landlord, but as a new tenant. I make it seem like it was purchased by a corporation and I am a new tenant. That way I can keep a better eye on my tenants by living next to them without them knowing who I am. Because things may get personal, I want to have the ability to use another member of my team to act as a property manager to do the evictions if necessary without breaking a new 'friendship'.

I have found it very beneficial to play the game from the inside out. I have also done the traditional approach of announcing myself as the landlord and that has worked as well. You can test it out to see which method you feel works best for you. The ultimate goal is to make sure you are running a tight ship. Make sure people are paying on time, the property is being well taken care of by the tenants and well attended to by your property manager.

Trying to be kind and compassionate, Mr. Nice Guy or Ms. Sweet Gal allowing tenants to pay you partial rent and pay exceptionally late, be mindful that the bank is still expecting their mortgage from you to be paid on time. Whatever monies you don't collect, you will then be paying out of pocket. The mortgage stubs come every month and by not collecting full payments on time, you are essentially paying for other adults to live.

Your property is an asset. It will be something that attracts other buyers, and it can be leveraged as cash or a line of credit. Take care of it so it maintains its value. Making upgrades to the property over time will help increase or maintain the value. Treat the property like money in the bank.

"This can be the start of an anchor for your family legacy."

In closing, you have made a major accomplishment and attained the "American Dream" of homeownership. You are to be commended and should be very proud of yourself. But...as with any great reward, there may be hiccups. Don't fret. The reward is far greater than the challenges. "To whom much is given, much is required".

May you create many amazing memories in your new home and may it be the first of many; each bigger and better than the last.

To Learn More from Jay Morrison Visit
www.JayMorrisonAcademy.com

About the Author

Jay Morrison, also known as "Mr. Real Estate", is an international real estate developer, author, TV personality, entrepreneur and human rights activist. Jay is the CEO and founder of the Jay Morrison Brand which is the parent company to Jay Morrison Real Estate Partners, a real estate development firm and the Jay Morrison Academy, an online real estate investor's school and mentorship program.

Despite being a high school dropout, an at risk youth and three-time felon, Jay made a major life transformation for the better over a decade ago that not only made him a millionaire before the age of 30 but also propelled him into the national spotlight. He now uses his life experiences and personal story of triumph to empower and impact the lives of thousands of his Academy students, troubled youth, ex-offenders and real estate professionals throughout the world.

CPSIA information can be obtained
at www.ICGtesting.com
Printed in the USA
LVOW13s0443080217
523559LV00006B/142/P